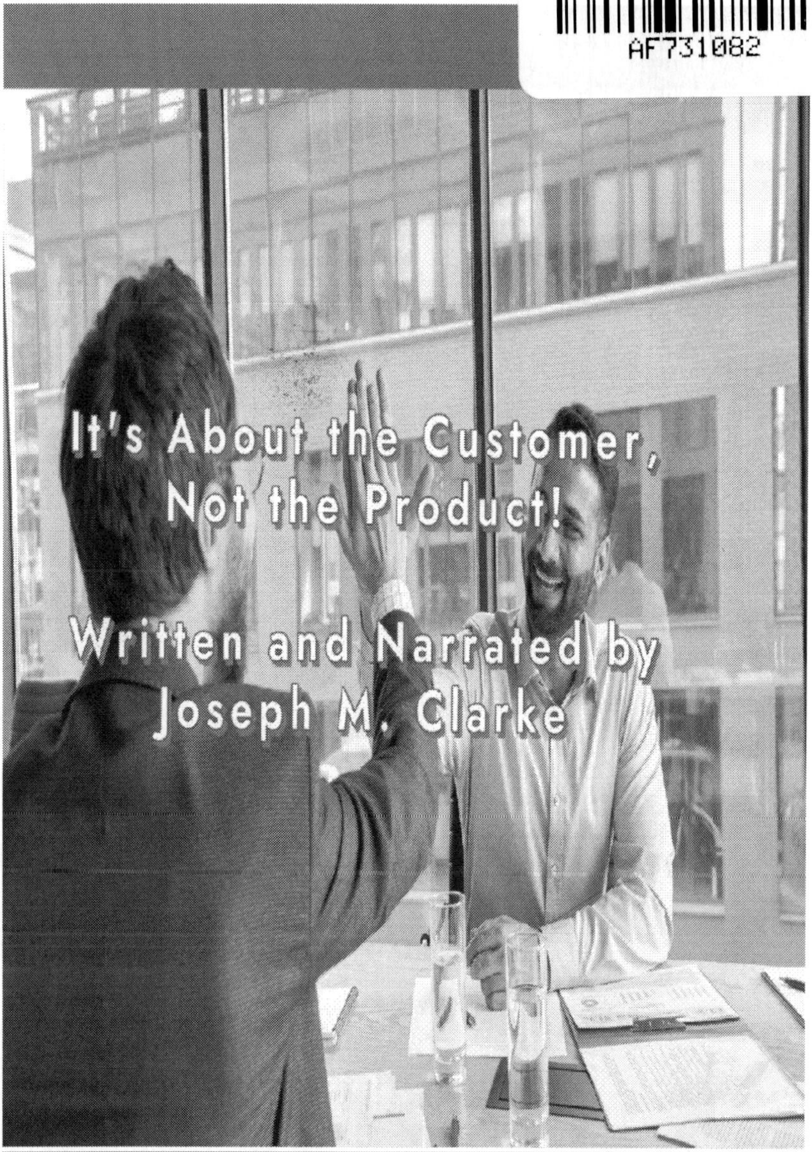
It's About the Customer,
Not the Product!
Written and Narrated by
Joseph M. Clarke

Joseph M. Clarke

ISBN: 978-1-960321-06-0

Introduction

Before I begin, I want to thank you for taking the time to read or listen to this book! I know as a salesperson, your time is valuable, and I promise not to waste it!

I have been in sales my entire life. From the time I was twelve to when I retired a few years ago at 57, I have sold everything from newspapers to matches and mailing machines to medical supplies. I have led sales teams from six to six hundred and more.

In my career in sales, I have learned a few things. In this book, I will give you helpful tips on how to build relationships, sell value and solutions, and sell profitably while providing value for your customers.

Almost every salesperson spends many hours driving. At one point in my life, I covered half the state of Arizona, from with Phoenix to the border with Mexico from north to south, and from New Mexico to California from East to West. I drove over 60,000 miles a year. It occurred to me during one of those long drives that I needed to put my time to better use. Now this was before the internet and cell phones, so I decided to make cassette tapes to listen to. I made tapes of sales presentations of the products that I wanted to focus on, tapes to review the features, advantages, and benefits of the individual products, etc. I saw immediate benefits to this, not only in my knowledge of the products but in the quality of my sales calls. I then began to listen to tapes on selling. From Zig Zigler to Dennis Waitley, I started really analyzing where I could do better. I was honored to be named the Rookie Sales Rep of the Year that year. It laid the foundation for a very profitable and rewarding career in sales.

That is my goal with this audiobook! To share with you what I have learned over a 35+ year career in bite sizes chapters in the hope that you will take time while driving to hone your craft and build and improve your skills!

I hope you enjoy the journey, and that, along the way, I can provide a blueprint that will allow you to build better relationships with your customers, sell more, increase profitability, and increase your job satisfaction!

Let’s get started!

Chapter 1

What is the Difference between Relationship Selling and Other types of Sales?

What pops into your head when you hear the term Relationship Selling? Do you envision a "Major Account" Sales position where you're schmoozing a client over an expensive meal with the hope of signing a multi-million-dollar contract? Or perhaps a slick car salesman with great closing skills to "get you to sign on the bottom line? Well, although both roles may have relationship skills, for purposes of his book, that is not what we are focusing on.

Selling in its most basic form is fairly straightforward. Selling is the ability to understand your customer's needs and provide a solution to that need in a manner that provides value to your customer and profitability to the company that is employing better than your competitors can. Sounds easy, right?

Relationship selling is the ability to know the

customer well enough to understand the customer's needs better than your competitors do. And by knowing the customer's needs better, your solution is better! By knowing precisely what your customer values, your presentations are customized to what matters to him or her! And when the customer hears the presentation in a way that solves his or her problems, they have infinitely more trust that your product or service will solve their problems. Why? Because they feel as if they've been heard! They believe you "get it"!

Let's look at an example in our lives. I'm going to use getting your car repaired for some mechanical problem. Stay with me!

So, you take your car in for one of those "mystery problems". You just hope you can replicate it when you get to your mechanic. You're trying to explain what is going on, but you're not really sure if the mechanic understands. Then they ask a few questions, and you almost shout: "That's it!!!!" You get it! That's the feeling you want your customer to have!

So, as we start to talk about Relationship Building, your intent is a crucial component as you prepare your sales calls. Is your goal aligned with building a relationship, or do you just "want to get the business"? Are you looking for opportunities to show your customer that "you get them," or are you caught up in talking about the features of your product, or worse, how bad your competition is?

In the Book "7 Habits of Highly Effective People", Steven Covey talks about intent. One of the strong statements that he states is very simple, and it is a game changer! The saying goes: "Start with the end in mind".

So, make a commitment to yourself today! I am going to shape my calls with the end goal of having the best relationship I can with my customers!

Chapter 2
Setting the Stage

This is a quick chapter designed to clarify the selling situation this book is designed to address.

There is a multitude of different sales positions. There are retail sales positions, positions that spend much of the day making cold calls. Many positions, especially entry-level positions that have large geographic territories selling business equipment or business services. These positions are a great way to break into sales and allow you to learn how to present a product and manage a territory.

If you have been in one of these positions, you know that almost all of the training you receive from these companies is about the product. Features, Advantages, Benefits. Training in leasing, purchasing, and service contracts. But guess what? Most companies in this type of industry do little or no focus on the customer! So that transition to the next level leaves a gap that must be addressed if you are going to be successful.

The remainder of this book will focus on those sales positions where the interaction with a relatively small group of customers over a long period of time. Years in fact. So, the determining factor of whether you are mediocre or great shifts from your ability to present a product to how well you develop your relationship.

Now that we've cleared that up, let's get down to the meat of the matter!

Chapter 3
Getting off on the Right Foot

Let's set the stage:

You've been given a new customer, and you want to get off on the right foot. So, what do you do?

What do you know about the company and the customer? Do any of your other customers know him or her? Have you checked out their profile on LinkedIn?

Any research you can do on the customer will go a long way in developing a strategy to develop your image and your relationship. For example, has the customer been with his company for a long time or a short time. How is the company positioned relative to their competitors? What industry is the company in? What challenges does that industry face? All this background will result in you having a plan to demonstrate to the customer that you are prepared to learn how to be an asset to them and their company.

Notice I said, "learn"!

One of the biggest mistakes many salespeople make is the belief that they have all the answers. How can you have the answers when you haven't even asked the questions yet?

Next, you want to meet the customer. Always call to make an appointment! Most of you are thinking, "Duh"! But if I had a dollar for every time a rep wanted to "Stop by and introduce myself" unannounced. I could have retired even earlier!

Remember, everything you do, especially at the beginning of building a relationship, sends a message to your customer. Walking in unannounced sends the message that you don't respect their time. Asking via a call or email for an opportunity to meet them and learn about them and their company sends the message that you respect them and have the willingness to learn. For building a foundation of a long-term business relationship, that is gold!

Chapter 4

Preparation for the Introduction Meeting

To ensure that this very important meeting begins the relationship on the right foot, it is essential that you prepare!

To begin, ask yourself how much you know about the relationship between your customer and the company that you represent.

Do you know the current book of business that your customer purchases through your company?

Is that book of business growing or shrinking?

How is your company viewed about your competition? Is your company the "go to" company of the "backup"?

How profitable is the current book of business?

Why does the customer purchase these items through your company?

Is this book of business under a contract? If so, how

long is the contract term?

Under what conditions did the previous representative from your company leave the account? Was he or she viewed positively in the account?

Is the customer paying within the terms of the contract?

Are there other competitors in the account that are selling the same product line that you are? If so, do they have the majority or the minority of the business?

Are there credits or returns that are unresolved? If so, can you resolve these issues before your appointment?

Are there any pending orders that are due to be delivered? If so, are they on time? If not, has the customer been informed of the delay?

Is the customer that you are meeting with the sole decision maker? If not, who else is important in the decision-making process?

These are just a few of the important questions that you want to answer for yourself before you meet with your customer!

Your sales manager should be able to help. You can review all data on sales reports that are available to you. Calling the manufacturing or credit department to discuss the account will also help. And, of course, if the previous rep is available, he or she will be invaluable.

As you start to create a picture of "the lay of the land", it will help you develop an agenda for the first meeting. Let's go through a sample of an agenda!

So, after doing your homework, is your contact at this company likely to have a positive, negative, or neutral view of your company?

If the view is negative, do you know why? If there are problems, try very hard to understand and solve the most pressing problems. Starting a meeting with someone that doesn't view your company in the best light with 2-3 things that you have already resolved will go a long way toward neutralizing any animosity that simmers with the customer. Also, understand that, depending on the type of problem and history, your goals are different with an angry customer than a customer that views your company positively. Your goals are to be considered as part of the solution, not part of the problem!

So, apologize for the past issues, ask what further you can do to resolve any issues, and ask for an opportunity to help them achieve their goals within the products or services your company offers. And ask for the opportunity to meet with them again! As the saying goes, “Kill them with Kindness”. This attitude and persistence will almost certainly neutralize the negative image of your company!

Now, let’s discuss an account that views your company positively. With the same due diligence as we previously discussed, you will hopefully have found a few, if any, issues that need resolution. So, in this scenario, let the customer know you have reviewed the current business. And then THANK THEM! If you did not discover any current issues that were unresolved, ask the customer if they are aware of any pending samples, orders, product demonstrations etc., that need addressing.

Also, in reviewing your current book of business, are there any "gaps" in the purchasing portfolio? Almost all products belong to a "family" of products and services purchased together. Is your "family" of products intact?

Finally, in your review of the product portfolio, is any business at risk? You can almost guarantee that your competitors have been trying very hard to get your business during the transition of representation. If you are concerned about the risk of losing any part of your product portfolio, prepare to address it with the customer!

Finally, what about the neutral customer? Most of the time, this customer doesn't dislike your company. They just don't view them as highly as other competitors.

Here, your job is to find out "why"! The ability to determine if this is product-based, contract-based, or relationship-based will give you a roadmap for how to proceed.

This may be the “hardest” scenario to know for certain how to proceed. Why? Because, more often than not, the customer will not fully disclose the real motivation behind his attitude toward your company.

Chapter 5

Remember this above all else when meeting a new customer:

When you are asking a customer to buy from you, many if not most of the time, you are asking them to STOP buying that product from someone they trust and more than likely have a good relationship with.

Think about that for a minute!

How do we as human beings react when asked to take something from a friend? It creates a level of anxiety and what is called "cognitive dissonance", which means we as humans justify our actions when there is a conflict between what we feel and how we behave.

Let me give an all-too-common example:

You are calling on a client with a product that has a lower price than what the account is currently buying. But the competitor is a large supplier that has a long history with the client. Sound familiar? If their role in the company is to procure products, the client is met with a dilemma. His or her role is to save the company money by purchasing the best value for the company.

Notice I said value and not price. We will talk more about this later, but it is the value that your product or service provides that matters. While price is a part of the value proposition, if it is the only part you are presenting, you won't get very far.

But for the purposes of this example, let's pretend the value is superior to your competitor.

What will your customer do? Because he is faced with the scenario of taking business from a trusted supplier with he or she has a great relationship with, many times, they will do one of the following:

1. Nothing. Depending on a multitude of circumstances, the decision maker will decide to table the item. They may state that "it's not a big deal in the big picture," that they have "bigger fish to fry," etc. This procrastination is many times precisely because of the existing relationship they have with the current supplier.
2. Your customer will tell you the product did not meet

the needs of his company. Whether this is indeed the case or simply an excuse for not moving the business will be hard to determine. The key in this situation is to remember that the relationship you create will take time, tenacity, and patience.

3. They will bring your proposal to the existing supplier and ask them to meet the price or value of your proposal. This surprises and frustrates many new sales reps. However, if you see this behavior, and your customer demonstrates loyalty to a vendor, you can point out that you brought value to his company, even if he didn't give you the business. If you continue down this path, you will gain goodwill and business opportunities, perhaps from another company, your customer doesn't have the same level of loyalty.

This "cognitive dissonance" is precisely why product-centric sales training fails if the customer-centric approach is not included!

So, as we get ready to meet our customer for the first time, remember to "Start with the end in mind"!

Chapter 6
The initial appointment (Finally!)

The biggest mistake I see reps making, especially new reps, is not listening.

Hard to believe, isn't it?

It isn't that they don't want to listen.

The problem is that they are so focused on what they are going to say, remembering the features, etc., that they don't have their brain focused on the customer.

And if they are focused on the words the customer is saying, they are not focused on all the other information the customer is communicating.

Have you ever been reading a book and you get to the end of a page and realize that you don't remember what you just read? It's not that you weren't looking at the words, is it? Instead, it was that your mind was thinking about something else!

It's the same in sales. If your internal attention, that is, what you are thinking about, is not focused completely on your customer, you are missing key information and buying cues.

So, in this initial appointment, it is vital that you "tune in" completely to both the verbal and non-verbal information your customer is providing.

You've done your research on the company and the history between your company and your customer. You've researched your customer on LinkedIn and maybe spoken to other mutual acquaintances to learn about them. Now all you need is an agenda, the talking points you want to cover in this first meeting. As the saying goes, you only get one chance to make a first impression!

In this agenda, the topics to cover should be in the form of a question. "Asking" rather than "telling" communicates to the customer several important attributes about you. Asking implies that you want to learn. What the customer is telling you is important, and you want to provide value to their company and make his job easier. So, as you frame these questions, make sure you are communicating this in the way you ask the question, and handle the answer!

Let's take a look at two examples using the same set of data so I can illustrate what I mean:

You are about to call on Tom Smith. He's been with the company you are calling on for five years. His title is Purchasing Manager. Your company does $200,000 per year in sales. Your competitor does significantly more business. In preparing for the sales call, you have learned that the business is down 30% from the previous year. You have also learned that a pending order is delayed by 3 weeks, but you are not sure whether that has been communicated. The account has not been called on for 6 weeks during the transition period. The company is publicly traded, and the stock price is down, as are sales. In calling for the appointment, you were told that Mr. Smith was very busy and that he had to reschedule twice because he was interviewing for a Purchasing Agent.

A lot going on, right? This should be fun!

In the first example, let's see how framing a question can make a huge difference in what is being communicated and how the customer receives that.

After thanking Mr. Smith for the opportunity to meet with him, you get to work on your questions. Here are three that you lead with:

"I'm new to your account, so I was hoping you could tell me about how our company is performing for you?"

"It's been over a month since you were called on, is there anything that you are aware of that needs to be taken care of?"

"Are there any projects that you're currently working on that my company can help you with?"

So, what do you think? Are these good questions, or could they be improved?

Let's look at a different way of asking the same type of questions:

"Mr. Smith, in preparing for our meeting today, I noticed that you've been a great customer for several years. I also noticed that over the past year, our business has fallen off. Would you mind explaining how our company is perceived by you as a supplier?"

"As part of my preparation, I did notice a current

order in the system, so thank you! I also noticed that the order is delayed by a few weeks because of supply issues that are wreaking havoc on all of us. I wanted to make sure that the delay had been communicated and that you had the new shipping information?"

"I had the opportunity to view your profile on LinkedIn. I noticed a post you had made about the need for automation in the supply chain. In reviewing the account records, I noticed that your company is not taking advantage of some of the efficiencies that my other customers are. I was wondering if we could explore how to help our companies work more efficiently together?"

"To help me learn about how to be more valuable to your company, I would like to schedule a business review. I'd like to learn what are some areas we can improve upon so that we can help your company reach your strategic goals.

Would that be of interest to you?"

Both sets of questions seek information from Mr. Smith, but the second set of questions communicates so much more about YOU!

One more thing: How you respond to the answers is as important as asking the question!

If the question is worth asking, then what you do with the answer is to communicate something to the customer.

In our question about whether a shipping delay was communicated, depending on the answer, you might have to get clarification on other people to communicate to, steps that will have to be taken, etc.

Also, make sure to take notes. It's surprising to me how often I have seen salespeople not taking notes in a meeting. I have had reps tell me that they feel taking notes makes the meeting "too formal". I disagree! Taking notes means that what the customer is saying is important! Simply stating, "If it's alright with you, I want to take a few notes to make sure I have a list of everything to do after we finish the meeting."

There is a saying:

"Don't tell me how much you know until you show me

how much you care."

Use your questions to communicate about you and the value you put on the relationship!

Chapter 7

Find out what is important

As we've discussed in the last chapter, every sales call should be "choreographed" to improve the relationship between you and your customer. And that relationship should be improved in both a business and personal relationship.

Let's discuss how that might take place:

On a business level, many customers are publicly traded companies. As such, there are numerous sources of information about the company. Stock prices, earnings, sales growth information, and more is available in the news, on the internet, and in industry trade groups. Becoming familiar with these sources and regularly keeping up to date on the latest news, trends, and activities will educate you about the pressures that your customer is facing. In addition to your customer, you should also know their competitors and follow them as well.

If you are new to the industry, try to subscribe to any

industry publications that are available. It will educate you on industry trends, government news that is relevant to that industry, and any mergers or consolidations that are currently happening.

Also, learn if there are annual trade shows that take place or professional chapters that meet monthly or quarterly. If so, ask if you can join as a vendor member and attend the meetings. This is a great opportunity to spend time with your customer outside of the office!

As you review the data and news, be especially focused on opportunities to discuss how your company could provide solutions based on this news. Solutions such as automation, innovation, financial terms, and inventory streamlining are just a few of the solutions that your company may be able to provide that have little to do with the "product" itself. But the timely introduction of the "value adds" will change how your customer views you and your company. When you transform your image from a "vendor" or "supplier" to a "strategic partner," you have come a long way to building the foundation for a strong relationship. It won't happen overnight, but setting the tone early will allow you more access to your customers' time and will be a major consideration in choosing a partner to deal with!

On the personal side, the focus should be on the customers' business goals and anything you can connect with them in their nonbusiness personal life.

Here the sources are almost limitless. With social media, and professional organizations such as the Rotary Club, Chamber of Commerce, Trade Organizations, and more, you should be able to learn a lot about your customer's ambitions, expertise, and career path in a short time. All this background gives you topics to learn about. And as you learn and discuss this with your customer, you are building the foundation of a strong relationship.

On social media, LinkedIn is a great source to learn about your customer and any groups he or she belongs to. You should follow your customer on that sight and any others to understand what initiatives within their industry are important to them. If they are actively posting on a topic, try to learn as much as you can about it. And if they are receiving accolades, obviously, you will want to congratulate them.

If you meet with your customer in their office, you should notice anything on the walls, their desk, or credenza that gives you insight into their family, hobbies, and interests. Take the time, even if it is a few minutes to try to engage the customer in something aside from work. If there is an activity or interest that you are not familiar with, take some time before the next meeting to educate yourself on the sport or activity. Relating to your customer on that topic in a way that the customer realizes that you took the time to learn about something important to them will communicate that he or she is important to you and your career, but also that you value the relationship enough to invest in it!

One final word on this topic before we move on:

The interest that you have in the topics and the willingness to learn about your customer must be genuine. Pretending to be interested will do more harm than good. Your ability to show your customer that you want to learn about them and their business will create the opportunity to differentiate you from your competition and, more importantly, align your goals with that of the customer. Once you've done that, selling becomes much more enjoyable!

Chapter 8

Walk the Walk

During my career in Sales, I was fortunate enough to spend 16 years as an outside sales manager with teams of varying sizes from 6 to 60 reps. One of the things I tried to do with all customers is to meet regularly, from quarterly to annually, to review the relationship and outline any areas of concern or opportunities.

I can tell you with 100% certainty that the #1 complaint that I heard during my career was that reps didn't follow through with promises. In other words, they "Talked the talk but didn't walk the walk".

I want you to take just a moment and put yourself in the customer's position:

You had the chance to meet with your customer. Quite honestly, he or she was impressed with your preparation and enthusiasm. But before they can trust you with a portfolio of business, you must prove to them that you can handle it in a way that builds trust.

So, they may give you a project they want you to work on. Or they may ask you a question about something. They may genuinely want to know the answer. But, at the same time, they are testing you to determine if you will respond and how!

During every call, anything that is agreed upon as an action item, whether it is something that the customer wants you to do or something that you asked the customer to do: WRITE IT DOWN!

Writing something down while you are on the call communicates to the customer that you have the follow-up skills to assure that things will get done. For example, writing down what the customer agrees to do and then asking about it on the next call communicates to the customer the item that you are following up on is important.

I encouraged the reps I worked with to start each sales call (after some greeting, of course) to follow up on any action item from the previous call. It can be as simple as "At our last meeting, you asked me to follow up on a credit that you thought was due. After talking to our accounts payable, they sent me a copy of the credit memo that we issued. So, I made a copy for your records."

We also discussed the opportunity to provide a response to a bid that was coming out. I think you said that you were going to provide a copy of the bid for me to respond to. I was wondering if you were able to have that for me?"

Showing your customer that you can handle the "little things" allows you the opportunity to ask to grow your business with their account!

Chapter 9
Don't be an Ostrich!

The second most common complaint of customers is that the reps "shy away" from a problem. While this is similar to a lack of follow-up, it is different in that there is more emotion (anger, frustration) and a higher sense of urgency. So, your ability to handle these problems and how you handle them will communicate a lot of information to your customer.

Depending on how your company is structured, someone else in your company may find out about a problem before you do. If so, your company must have an infrastructure that allows you, as the relationship manager of the account, to be aware of problems and when and how they are resolved.

Problems come in all shapes and sizes. Credits, pricing, quality, IT, and delivery issues are just a few of the problems that arise with customers. Your ability to handle these problems and communicate the progress and resolution of the problem will determine how the customer views you and your company.

Here are some questions that you should ask to determine how to proceed:

1. Get as many details as you can of the specifics of the problem. Order #, date, item, and specifics are a must.
2. Is this problem an ongoing problem, or is it a solitary event?
3. Who is the person closest to the problem? (Especially important if the problem is a quality problem). Could I possibly speak with the person directly to find out exactly how to resolve this?
4. Do you need an answer immediately, or can I get back to you within three days?
5. If the problem is ongoing, ask to set a short meeting or call with the stakeholders for your customer and the appropriate people within your company to fix the problem. Ask yourself, "is this a people issue"? Meaning, is there someone within either organization that needs additional training? If not, is there a

process issue on either side? Your role is to advocate for your customer while creating a fix for both sides if you can do this in a collaborative way, you will earn a lot of respect from your customer.

6. After the call or meeting, make sure you follow up with your customer to ensure the issue is resolved.

Finally, don't deflect blame! If you made a mistake, apologize, and move on. The customer doesn't expect you to be perfect. Mistakes that are handled with an apology and resolution are accepted and appreciated. The key is to hit the problem head-on. The longer it sits out there, the more harm it does to the relationship!

Chapter 10

It's almost never about price alone!

As you move through the stages of building a relationship with your customers, the fruit of that effort will appear as you begin to negotiate to win business.

Your customer's job is to procure the supplies he or she needs at the best value for the company. But value does not equal just price. And if you have done a good job in building your relationship, you will have learned how to build value into your proposal in a way that makes sense to your customer!

This is where you need to be the student and the teacher! As a student, you should have learned (or asked to learn) about not only the product but also how to add value to your proposal. Adding payment terms, logistical efficiencies, product education and training, or being able to demonstrate real savings, a unique feature of your proposal, are just a few of the ways you can build value. So, the more you know about the "things that keep your customer up at night", the more value you can bring above and beyond the price.

Let's talk through an example to demonstrate what I mean:

I spent most of my career in medical supply sales. We had thousands of items to offer to our customers. The customers cared about quality, price, payment terms, distribution capabilities, contract compliance, and more. So, it was essential to know which parts of the puzzle the customer valued most when awarding the business. For our example, let's choose distribution capabilities. Unless I had a complete understanding of their internal supply chain, I knew it was imperative to understand their business and be prepared to customize my offering to provide efficiencies and solutions to any pain points they have (and all customers have pain points!)

This was almost never in the proposal. In addition, most of the time, the person handling the negotiation wasn't close enough to the day-to-day problems to truly provide the detail needed to understand where my company could help.

So, I did my own version of "Undercover Boss"!

By spending a few days shadowing the receiving and internal distribution process, I could provide much more value than the price the customer was asking for on a proposal. Even if my price was not the lowest, I also knew that if I could take away more internal costs than the difference in my price and my competitor's price, the value I was bringing would be viewed as superior! Very rarely does your customer want the best price. Instead, they want the best value.

So, in this example, I could demonstrate my company's ability to build orders in a way that allowed the customer to receive and handle the order in 33% less time than they were currently doing. By understanding their billing system, I reduced Accounts Payable effort by 25%. And by incorporating IT efficiencies, I reduced billing errors by 50%.

But the most important thing was that I

demonstrated to the customer that I was a strategic partner they could lean on to make their business operate better.

So, while I sold millions of dollars in products, the solutions often had little to do with why customers chose my company as their partner.

Conversely, if you can educate your customer on things that are going on in the industry and how those things affect the cost build-up of an item, the more understanding, and trust you will build with your customer.

For example, many of the products that I sold were made with cotton. So, part of my job as a rep, and a manager, was to educate my customers on the cost of cotton in times when the cotton output worldwide was very low. Having third-party indexes and articles to provide helped my customers understand what was happening in the world that affected the products they purchased. In addition, having solutions or alternatives to the products that helped them mitigate negative cost factors aligned me with the customer to try to find solutions that would be acceptable. Even if the customer didn't accept the alternatives, they understood the impact and appreciated the way the discussion was handled.

There are so many variables that make up any proposal. The purpose of this chapter is to remind you that if you work with your customer collaboratively to understand and address these variables when negotiating, you will understand how to put the most meaningful proposal in front of your customer and ultimately provide the best value!

Chapter 11

Stay Real

If you're listening to this book, there's a good chance you've invested in your career using other books to learn skills to advance your career. Since we just touched on negotiating with your customer, Let's discuss some of the books on negotiating skills that are available.

I've attended and taught negotiation skills for over 20 years. I believe there is great value in understanding "how the game is played". But equally important is understanding when different types of negotiation interaction work in your industry.

Many of the books on negotiations deal with one-time sales, such as real estate transactions. Many of the strategies that are taught involve the back and forth on finalizing the price. Terms such as "playing hardball", being willing to "walk away", and "red herring" are all strategies to create doubt in either the buyer or seller that the terms are acceptable.

It's important to understand these principles and

strategies, if for no other reason than knowing when someone is trying to use these strategies while negotiating with you.

But within the relationship selling that we have been discussing, a scenario where one party wins and the other loses never works for the long term.

If you have built a strong relationship with your customer, the trust they have in you and your company allows you to negotiate with them in a win-win style that allows honest discussions on how to build value, as we discussed before.

So, resist any strategies that feel harmful to the relationship. Also, resist any advice to "bait and switch". It almost always creates ill will.

If you find you are in a situation where you can't meet the terms of the customer, rather than "playing hardball", ask him or her if there is any part of your proposal that doesn't really provide value based on their situation. By taking away something the customer doesn't value, you may be able to reduce your cost and provide value in a way the customer cares about.

You can also ask for more time. Explaining to the customer that you want to talk to your management team to see if there are efficiencies you had not considered that would allow you to adjust your proposal signals flexibility and a desire to work with your customer. More importantly, the way you handle impasses in the negotiations will keep the relationship on solid footing and won't erode the trust you have built.

So "stay real" with your customer while negotiating. Leave the games to other industries and situations that don't value or require a relationship!

Say Thanks

Any success I have achieved in sales was because someone was willing to give me an opportunity to earn their business. Whether it was because they liked my work ethic or because I was able to learn what really mattered to them, the bottom line is "all things being equal, they wanted me to have the business," and for that, I was and still am grateful!

In my first year selling medical supplies, I was honored to have won "Rookie of the Year". I was both thrilled and humbled!

When I returned home from the sales meeting, I bought Thank You cards for my customers. My intent was not to brag about the award but to sincerely thank them for the opportunities I received to grow my business, how appreciative I was for that, and the impact it had on my family and me!

So, I encourage you to thank your customer for opportunities. Even if you don't win the business, thank your customer. And, while you are at it, ask them if there is anything you can improve upon in your proposal that would help you next time.

The key is this: If your customer wants you to succeed and is vested in your success, you are way ahead of the game! Now all you have to do is find a way to provide value in a way that is meaningful to your customer's business!

I hope you have enjoyed this book. And I hope that in some small way, this will help you in your selling career by increasing both your success and earnings and your job satisfaction. Please feel free to send questions and comments to my email: jclarke@clarkecommunicationsllc.com.

Thanks for taking the time to listen to this book!

Now go out and sell!!!!

Made in United States
Troutdale, OR
11/03/2026

56844363R00029